STORIES OF THE BOY JESUS

- In the Beginning
- The Birth of Jesus
- Jesus Growing Up Years

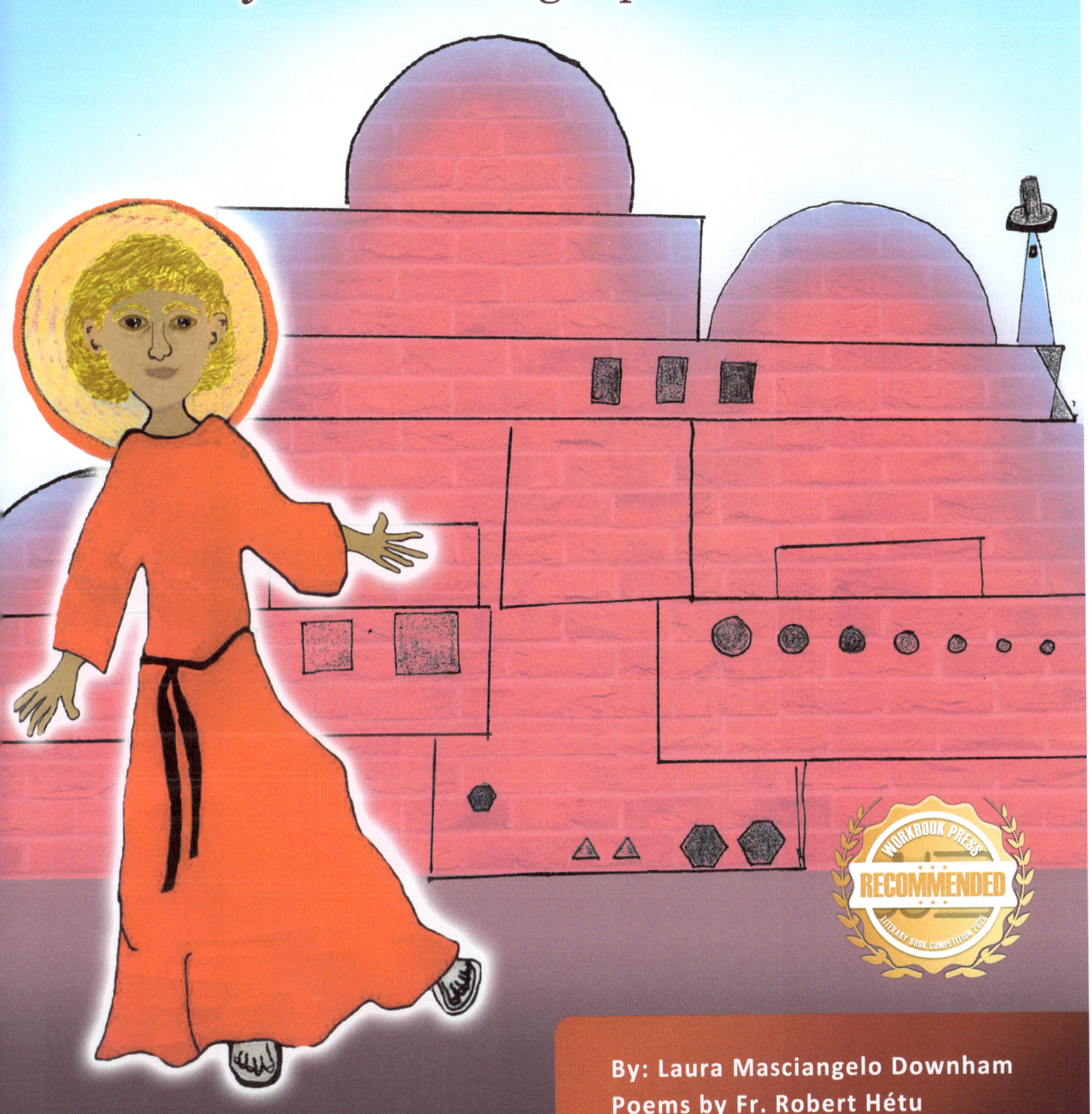

By: Laura Masciangelo Downham
Poems by Fr. Robert Hétu

WORKBOOK PRESS LLC

187 E Warm Springs Rd,

Suite B285 Las Vegas NV 89119 USA

Website: https://workbookpress.com/

Hotline: 1-888-818-4856

Email: admin@workbookpress.com

Ordering Information:

Quantity sales. Special discounts are available on quantity purchases by corporations, associations, and others. For details, contact the publisher at the address above.

ISBN-13:   978-1-963718-80-5   Paperback Version

978-1-963718-82-9   Digital Version

978-1-963718-85-0   Hardback Version

REV. DATE: 08/21/2024

STORIES
OF THE BOY
JESUS

(There are three parts to this book)

In the Beginning

The Birth of Jesus

Growing Up Years

STORIES
OF THE BOY
JESUS
(In The Beginning)

By: Laura Masciangelo Downham
Poems by: Fr. Robert Hétu

PREFACE

This book has been on my mind for many years, but more recently when I started to work with children in sacramental preparation, sadly they lacked the knowledge of God.

Children have all the questions a grownup has and much more. They would come to my class eager to know anything and everything about Jesus, Mary, Joseph, the Holy Trinity and some of the saints and angels. I wanted to begin the relationship between them in class. Some were informed by their parents but other children it was the first knowledge about Jesus, Mary, Joseph and the Holy Trinity. Fortunately those children who knew nothing let me know. On one occasion I gave out Rosaries to my class, and one young boy took the Rosary and decided to colour Mary's face. I stopped the boy and said, "Don't do that to that holy article, it's blessed by the priest and sacred." The young boy stood up and said to me, "Why don't you mind your own business," and continued to say, "Listen here, I don't want to be here, I don't want my first communion or any part of it, my parents are forcing me to come here. I do not know who God or Jesus are and I don't care to know." To make the story short, we resolved the concern and now he's a child of God, his view points in life are different now and not on a rough road any longer. Children should get to know about God before anything in their life. They need to know God is for them and wants to help in any way that the child should need. How does this work? You pray for your favour and then very quietly in God's time He will bless you with the grace you prayed for. Every request is different. "Ask and you shall receive", that saying is in the Bible.

In these books I'm trying to create roots between children and Jesus of where Jesus came from; how He was like as a young boy. None of us know this, so knowing children I created fictitious stories of what I think Jesus was like as a child. Book 1 and 2 are all about facts from the Bible and other religious books. Then in book 3 only, the stories are fictitious, which I believe could be the way Jesus was when He was a child. It's based on the way His adult life was like.

Parents and teachers: this sentence is for you; if you love these children, open the door for Jesus to them. This world is tough and the children need God in their lives to create a better future for them and for all.

Laura

Dedication

To my grandfather
Antonio Donato Bada

In the Beginning

The Boy Jesus

CONTENTS

INTRODUCTION

In this book are many stories of goodness and values for God's people. Jesus demonstrates to us in many ways of how He loves us. Jesus loves us so much that Jesus showed us the way when He came down to earth.

Some do acknowledge and accept His loving ways. Life holds an abundance of trials and tribulations. When we let Jesus into our lives, He helps us through it and life becomes less difficult.

In our journey through Life, we learn about The Holy Trinity as being God the Father, God the Son and God the Holy Spirit. The Holy Trinity is there for us at all times and anywhere to give us insight in our life's concerns.

THE HOLY TRINITY

The Theory Of An Apple

Three parts of an apple   **Three parts of God**

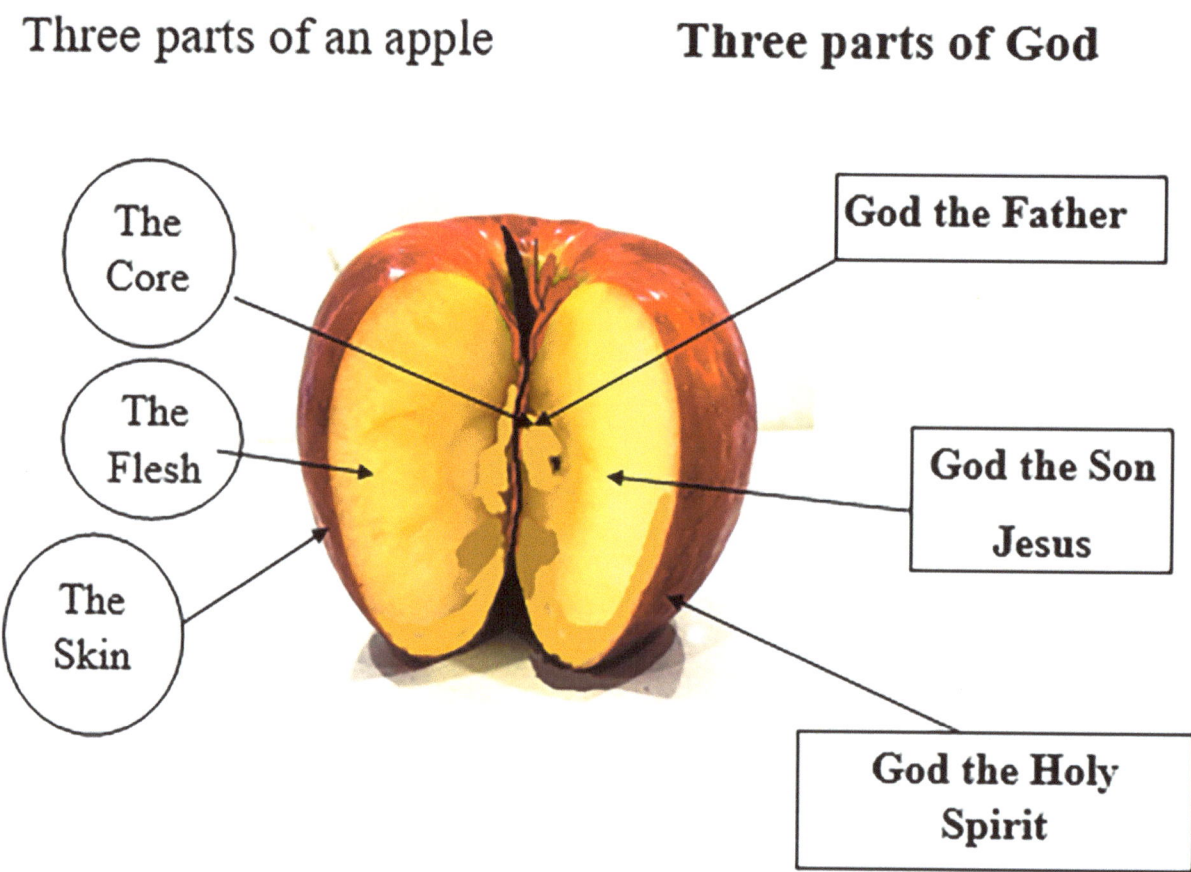

The Core

The Flesh

The Skin

God the Father

God the Son
Jesus

God the Holy
Spirit

This representation was shared with us by Father Robert Bulbrook in 2012 at St. Joseph Church Patron of Canada Parish in Acton, Ontario, Canada

THE STORIES ABOUT THE PROPHETS

It was foretold through the prophets a Messiah was coming. What is a prophet you ask? A prophet is someone inspired by God. It's a person who tells what will happen in the future.

There was a prophet in Jerusalem called Simeon, who was righteous and holy. He was waiting for the consolation of Israel and the Holy Spirit was upon him. It was revealed by the Holy Spirit that he would not die before he had seen the Messiah, also known as the Christ.

Prophet Simeon

There was also a prophetess, named Anna, a widow, who was very old, the daughter of Phanuel, from the tribe of Asher. She was 85 years old and never left the temple praying and fasting always. She was also waiting for our Saviour, Jesus Christ, the Son of God.

Anna the Prophetess

My Heart Is Ready

(Based on Psalm 57)

My heart is ready
My heart is ready, O Lord
I will sing Your praise

Shine on earth Your light
Above the heavens arise
My Lord and my God

Awake, lyre and harp
Yes, I will awake the dawn
I will thank You Lord

Among the people
Your love reaches the heavens
Your truth to the skies

Shine on earth Your light
Above the heavens arise
My Lord and my God

Fr. Robert Hétu

All Blessings Be Yours

(Inspired by 1 Chronicles 29: 10-13)

O loving Father
All blessings be Yours, my God
For eternity

Yours, Lord are grandeur
Power, majesty, splendour
And all glory too

For all in heaven
And on earth is Yours, O Lord
Now and for ever

You are exalted
All sovereignty is Yours Lord
You are head of all

Might, grandeur and strength
All power is in Your hands
Lead us to Yourself

Therefore, O dear God
We give You thanks and all praise
Holy is Your Name

Fr. Robert Hétu

THE STORY OF SAINT ANNE

St. Anne was born in Bethlehem and married Joachim from Nazareth in Galilee.

Joachim was a shepherd. He was given the task of supplying the temple of Jerusalem with sheep for sacrifices.

After twenty years of marriage, Anne and Joachim struggled to have children. When, on a feast day, Joachim presented himself and offered a sheep to sacrifice in the temple. He was hurt and troubled by a certain Ruben (a certain person). Joachim understood that men without any children were unworthy to enter into the temple.

Where upon Joachim, bowed down with grief and did not return home, but went to the country side, up the mountains, to be with God in solitude. Also, Anne having learned the reason for the prolonged absence of her husband, cried to God to bless her with a child, promising to dedicate the child to the service of God.

The angel told Anne at home, and then told Joachim while still on the mountains that they would have a child, a girl who shall be named Mary. When Mary was three years old St. Anne and St. Joachim gave Mary to the temple to be raised by the Temple of Jerusalem in fulfillment to her divine promise. St. Anne was said to be ninety two years old when she conceived Mary. Therefore she would have been around ninety-five when she gave Mary to the temple. Probably close to her time of death.

St. Anne and Mary as a child

Mary, she would have been around twelve years old or a little older at the time of the events described in the Gospel.

THE ANNUNCIATION

How did Jesus come to be? It all started when an Angel, the Angel Gabriel, sent by God from heaven went to a young girl named Mary (the future mother of Jesus) where she lived in Nazareth, a town in Galilee, over 2000 years ago. Now remember this is the same Mary who St. Anne gave birth to.

The Angel Gabriel went to her and said,

"Greetings, you are greatly favoured! The Lord is with you."

Mary was greatly troubled at his words and wondered what kind of greeting this might be.

But the angel continued to say to her,

"Do not be afraid, Mary, you have found favour with God. You will be with child and give birth to a son and you are to give Him the name Jesus."

"How will this be?" Mary asked the Angel, "Since I am a virgin pledged to be married to a man named Joseph."

The Angel answered,

"The Holy Spirit will come upon you and the Power of the Most High will overshadow you. So, the Holy One to be born will be called the Son of God, His name is Jesus, for nothing is impossible with God. Your cousin Elizabeth, who is very old and it was unable for her and her husband Zachariah to have a baby. God made it possible for her and is now in her sixth month."

"I am the Lord's servant," Mary answered. "May it be to me as you have said."

Then the Angel left.

Before this Mary was engaged to a man named Joseph, who found out Mary was pregnant, and so he was going to call the marriage off.

The Holy Spirit came upon Mary

JOSEPH'S DREAM

Read about this in the Bible: Matthew 1: 18-25

This is how the birth of Jesus Christ came about: His mother Mary was pledged to be married to Joseph, but before they came together, she was found to be with child through the Holy Spirit.

Because Joseph, her future husband was a righteous man and did not want to expose her to public disgrace, he had in mind to divorce her quietly.

But after he had considered this, an angel of the Lord appeared to him in a dream and said,

"Joseph son of David, do not be afraid to take Mary home as your wife, because Who is conceived in her is from the Holy Spirit. She will have a son and you are to name Him Jesus, because He will save the people from their sins."

The Angel Speaks To Joseph In A Dream

THE VISITATION

Very soon after, angel Gabriel told Mary about her being with child, the son of God to be named Jesus. Mary very quickly set out to a town called Hebron, up in the hill country of Judah.

Mary entered the home of Zachariah and Elizabeth. (Mary's cousins)

When Elizabeth heard Mary's voice, the baby inside Elizabeth's body jumped for joy.

Mary told Elizabeth what the angel had said to her about being with child. Her child will be the Son of God, which Mary needs to name Him Jesus.

Read about this in the Bible: Luke 1: 39-45

Mary Walking To Cousin Elizabeth's House

Mary continued to say,

"I had to come here today to see if the angel was correct in saying that you're with child too, but you have reached an age where you cannot conceive. How can this be? You are very old now and cannot bear any children."

Elizabeth said,

"Yes, I am too old, but with child. It is just as the angel said I am to have a son. A forerunner for Jesus and His name is to be called John." (Known later on as John the Baptist.)

"Anything is possible with God."

Blessed Virgin Mary

**Elizabeth, Mary's cousin,
John the Baptist's mother**

Open The Door Of Our Heart

The light of the daily sunrise
Is followed by the darkness of night
However, the warmth and light
Of the Rising Son never sets

The light of truth shines on us all
But if we close the blinds
Of the windows of our heart
We will be deprived of eternal light
If our heart is not awake the Lord will not knock
However, if our heart is watchful the Lord will gladly enter

Let us, open the door of our heart
Waiting and watching
And the King of Glory will enter
Sharing His gift of eternal light

Fr. Robert Hétu

STORIES
OF THE BOY
JESUS
(The Birth of Jesus)

By: Laura Masciangelo Downham
Poems by: Fr. Robert Hétu

CONTENTS

INTRODUCTION

In the story of Jesus' Birth, God placed us in the midst of a magnificent creation and ask only that we love Jesus and to love and respect each other with gratitude. God gave us the church to keep His message alive and interpret that message on the ever-changing human conditions until the end of time.

WHO IS GOD THE FATHER?

He is firstly our heavenly Father who created us through our parents. God the Father created Heaven and earth. He made everything perfect for this eternal plan so we could live with Him forever and God the Father, sent Jesus to shine and enlighten the way for us.

God loves us more than anyone could love us. God the Father is strict, powerful, and everlasting. He is our living God. God is Good and True. God made everything good in the beginning. God is Righteous, God is Holy, God is Glorious, and God is Almighty. God, the Father, is Eternal.

In judgement God is filled with mercy, but He has to be strict because some human beings cause much grief to humankind. He teaches us to correct sin, better our character, produce in us patience, and obedience. He loves us long before we loved Him.

The Power Of The Holy Spirit Comes
Through As A Dove

With God

(Inspired by a post on Twitter)

Without God, I have no purpose
Without God, I have no direction
Without God, I have no hope
Without God, I have nothing

With God, I have purpose
With God, I have direction
With God, I have hope
With God, I have everything

Amen

Fr. Robert Hétu

Augusta Caesar, Roman Emperor

BETHLEHEM

In the time of Joseph and Mary, there was political turmoil, the Roman power took over Israel politically. The Roman power ran Israel, not only Israel but all the countries of the world. Bethlehem included, but not the western world, for it was not discovered at the time.

At this point in time, Augusta Caesar was the emperor of Rome and wanted a census taken of all the people in the lands he had authority over. Everyone had to go back to the town of their ancestors and be registered.

Both Mary and Joseph went to Bethlehem be registered. Mary was pregnant by the power of the Holy Spirit and was travelling with Joseph her future husband. It was winter time at Bethlehem in December winters were milder and wetter with cool temperatures between 24 and 38 degrees F.

Joseph and Mary's hardships would have begun more than a week before the birth of Jesus, when the couple left their home in Nazareth in the northern highlands of Galilee, to register for the Roman census. It was not simple and it was assumed that Mary and Joseph likely would have travelled only ten miles a day because of Mary's impending delivery. She was nine months pregnant.

After walking for 90 miles, Mary and Joseph were trying to find a place, where they could rest. Mary was having great pain and close to delivering Jesus.

**Joseph And Mary On The Road
To Bethlehem**

27

THE BIRTH OF JESUS

The Birth of Jesus was planned for a long time by God the Father, nothing happens by accident with our Lord. God knows everything about everyone before it happens. Because of God's infinite love for us, He sent His Son to earth. The Blessed Mary, mother of Jesus, St Joseph, St. Anne, St. Joachim and even cousin Elizabeth and husband Zechariah, (the parents of John the Baptist) were all part of God's plan.

Mary was very tired and ready to give birth. Joseph couldn't find a place for her. There were no hospitals in those days.

Joseph finally found an inn, except the Innkeeper said the inn was full; but there was only the stable where the animals stayed. Joseph said that the stable would be fine. Mary gave birth there in the stable near the animals. Joseph made it very comfortable with a fire and he built a manager for Jesus, close to God's love. Jesus was born! Alleluia! Alleluia!

A Heavenly Miracle

On that first glorious Christmas day
As the Blessed Virgin Mary gave birth
A heavenly miracle came down to earth
The Son of God is born to show us the way

From a most humble, forlorn wooden stable
Humankind is forever full of divine grace
As we experience the Redeemer's sacred face
A saving gift for the world and all its people

Let us take time, this year, to open our heart
To remember the loving message of Jesus' birth
Promoting reconciliation and peace on earth
United and full of grace, let us do our just part

As the Blessed Virgin Mary gave birth
Yes, a heavenly miracle came down to earth

Fr. Robert Hétu

Nothing is impossible with God in your life.

The Angels of God danced around nearby fields and announced that the Son of God, named Jesus, was born.

All that stirring in the field, by the excited Angels, woke up the shepherds from their sleep. Hearing the Angels' message, the shepherds went in search for the Holy Family. They found them and went to visit them and told everyone what they saw.

King Herod

When King Herod, who was king of Judah, heard that Jesus was born, he was disturbed and all of his followers were fearful and angry. Then King Herod called together all the chief priests and teachers of the law and he asked them where the Christ was to be born?

"In Bethlehem in Judah," they replied. For this is what the prophets have said,

"But you Bethlehem in the land of Judah, are by no means least among the ruler of Judah; for out of you will come a ruler Who will be the shepherd of my people Israel." Matthew 1:6

King Herod

The Three Wisemen

King Herod called the Three Wisemen. One of them secretly found out the exact time that the star had appeared. King Herod sent them to Bethlehem and said, "Go and carefully search for the child and as soon as you find him report to me, so that I too may go and worship him." When the Three Wisemen saw the Star they were overjoyed and followed it until it came upon the stable.

Upon entering the stable where Jesus was born. The Three Wisemen saw the child with His mother Mary. They bowed down and worshipped Him. Then they opened their treasures and presented Jesus with gifts of gold, frankincense and myrrh.

The Wisemen were warned in a dream not to go back to King Herod, they returned to their country by another route.

When King Herod realized that he had been outwitted by the wisemen, he gave orders to kill all the boys two years old and younger in Bethlehem.

St. Joseph and the Dream

In the middle of the night, the Angel Gabriel told Joseph in a dream, to take Mary and the baby Jesus and escape from Bethlehem and go to Egypt. King Herod was trying to find and kill Jesus.

King Herod never found Jesus and after a few years he died.

After another dream, they left Egypt. Then Joseph took Mary and Jesus back to their hometown of Nazareth, where Jesus grew up.

O Blessed Joseph

(Inspired by a prayer of Pope Leo XIII)

O blessed Joseph, to you
    we confidently invoke
        your holy patronage

You are a man of dreams
    a man of action
        and foster father of Jesus

O watchful guardian
    of the Holy Family
        always gently guide us

As you humbly cared for
    Mary and the Child Jesus
        defend us in trial

With your power and strength
    assist us in our need
        continually coming to our aid

O blessed Joseph, to you
    we confidently invoke
        your holy patronage

Amen

Fr. Robert Hétu

By Grace

(Inspired by the Cursillo movement)

On that special weekend
We met our dear Lord
Now, we must study
And live in one accord

Let us put our service into action
And the sacraments to the fore
By grace overcoming obstacles
To become pious Christian leaders

Fr. Robert Hétu

STORIES
OF THE BOY
JESUS
(Jesus Growing Years)

By: Laura Masciangelo Downham
Poems by: Fr. Robert Hétu

CONTENTS

A Little

Live a little slower
Laugh a little louder
Smile a little longer
Love a little deeper
Pray a little harder

Fr. Robert Hétu

In the Small Village of Nazareth

In this tiny beautiful rugged isolated village called Nazareth made up about one thousand and six hundred people, in the days of Jesus. The people consist of farmers, fishermen, shepherds and a few wandering holy men.

The girls dressed simpler than boys, yet girls had more colourful clothing. Most men had beards and most women had long hair put in a bun at the back of their necks.

Jesus, Mary and Joseph were in Egypt when King Herod died. From Egypt Mary and Joseph took Jesus back to their home town of Nazareth where Jesus grew up.

Jesus played around the house with His cousins and friends in Nazareth. He knew everyone in town and possibly prayed in all their homes.

A view of the home in Nazareth, where Jesus, Mary and Joseph lived upstairs and the animals, which were for their food lived downstairs. They had a cow for milk and a bird for eggs, but they mostly ate vegetables, like beans and lettuce and for fruit grapes and oranges.

After dinner, usually with family and friends they spent two to three hours outside in conversation, but Jesus would go inside and prayed. The life of Jesus was already planned for Him before He was born. Jesus knew that He was on a mission from God the Father

Jesus, You Are Our Life

(Inspired by the intercessions of
Morning Prayer Sunday 1)

Jesus, You are our Life
And our Salvation
The Creator of the stars
The first Rays of the dawn

You are the Sun
That never sets
The true Light
That shines on everyone

May Your Holy Spirit
Teach us Your Way
May Your Wisdom
Guide us this day

Honoring Your Resurrection
We give You thanks
As we gather around the altar
Of Your Word and Body

From the depths of our hearts
We thank You for Your blessings
Jesus, You are our Life
And our Salvation
Amen

Fr. Robert Hétu

The Mission of Jesus

Right from a young lad Jesus knew He was on a mission from God the Father. His Father and our heavenly Father.

God wants us to know through Jesus that we all have to form a relationship with Jesus and that He is the way to a good life and to heaven.

When we were born, our mothers and fathers took care of us, or else we would have died. We depended on them for our safety and well-being, feeding us, and keeping us clean and healthy. God was there helping us too. At our birth God created each of us with a soul. We are all attached to Him believe it or not. God wants us to be happy and God sent His only Son Jesus to show us the way to happiness and how to live in this world and get to heaven.

God sent a Saviour called Jesus

When we get older, life steers us away from our mothers and fathers that we had depended on for so many years. As we grow into adulthood the demands of being human are much greater. It's much harder and there's no one to tell us right from wrong in our decision making. God loves us, He lives within us, all of us whether you like to know this or not. That's when you dig deep inside yourself and find God to guide you to the goodness of the world. You'll be guided to a life of brightness, a light shines inside you. God the Father, God the Son, Jesus, and God the Holy Spirit (The Holy Trinity) are with you taking good care of you with their gentle caring hands like your parents.

The Holy Trinity loves each and everyone of us, God has never left us since we were born. In your life there is a decision to be made. Do you make a good choice or a bad choice? God the Father cannot tell you which to pick. This is when the gift of Free Will was given to us by God. However, whatever choice you pick God will continue to love you whether you pick the right one or not. God loves you no matter what. The church is there to assist also with their holy men and women to lend aid and guide you, but cannot make the choice for you. Life is hard, but without God in your life, it is even harder.

JESUS FIRST DAY AT SCHOOL

Jesus woke up one morning as usual and readies Himself to go to school. He was six years old, very wise at this age, but was a human and as a human they have to go to school. He met up with His friends on the way to school and the children played and talked all the way to school. They talked about God the Father and God the Holy Spirit mostly. What they were like? What they expected from the people on earth? Who were the Saints and Angels in Heaven?

Jesus knew what everyone was thinking and doing everywhere at each moment of the day or night. Jesus lived a very quiet life as a child. So, He had to make sure He would not be discovered too early in His life for people would not take Him seriously.

At times children would ask Him to stop thinking or praying and come and play a game with them. After all, He was still a child in everyone's eyes. Jesus would say "not yet" and continued to pray or think.

It was Jesus first day at school and He went to the synagogue near where they lived. Some synagogues were run by priests and other synagogues were run by teachers. School was mostly for boys to attend classes of learning "The Book of Torah" a book of Bible stories and religious laws to abide by is what was being taught. Classes were everyday, girls were not permitted, except for some who came from rich families.

Jesus had many friends at school, everyone wanted to know everything about Him. They believed, in time without any questions, that He was the Son of God, made man (a human being). He brought them stories about our heavenly Father and what should be done on earth so that God's children could reside in heaven with our Lord God one day.

Jesus

When Jesus went to school there were no tables or chairs, everyone sat on the floor with mats. In their houses, they slept on the floor on their mats.

The Kingdom Of God

(Inspired by and based on Romans 14:17-19)

The Kingdom of God

Is not a matter of eating or drinking

But of justice, peace. and joy

Which is given by the Holy Spirit

Whoever serves our Lord Jesus

With loving and glad hearts

Pleases our heavenly Father

And receives the esteem of many

So then, let us make it our aim

To always work for peace

To strengthen one another

And give endless glory of God

The Kingdom of God

Is justice, peace. and joy

Fr. Robert Hétu

At the Beach

On one extremely hot sunny day at a beach on the north coast of Nazareth, Joseph and Mary took Jesus for a little relaxation to enjoy the day and sunshine. The Holy Family were so happy to be doing this. They walked mostly, but also brought their donkey to carry things.

After a few hours they reached the beach area and ran into the water to cool down. Then Jesus settled Himself upon a large mound of sand where He made sand birds.

Jesus walked around the beach to find coloured material to place on the sand birds. He found pink bark from a tree and yellow leaves at the foot of another tree. The birds looked so beautiful and real that Jesus let them fly. Jesus performed little miracles even as a child, but Jesus kept it a secret from everyone around Him.

Good Deeds, Food for Our Souls

On one occasion on a Friday around two thirty in the afternoon in the blazing sun. Jesus was walking to His house when He saw an old man, who could barely walk picking up rocks in front of His house. Jesus heard the old man praying for some help, so Jesus sent him two young boys to help him with the rocks. The two young boys said to the old man, "Dear old man do you need some help, we see you struggling."

The old man replied, "Yes I do, but I can't pay you, although you could have all my left over wood I have in the back from building my house.

The two young boys were happy with that and helped the old man. The two boys did a good deed and it shall be rewarded by God. These are known as good deeds and good deeds feed our souls.

Your House

(Inspired by and based on a homily of St. John Chrysostom Bishop)

Paint your house with the colours
Of gentleness and humility
Make your house radiant
With the light of justice

Decorate your house with the finest
Gold leaf of good deeds
Build your house with walls of generosity
On the rock-solid foundation of faith

Open the window of your heart
To the gift of the risen Son
Crown your house with
The pinnacle of prayer

Making your house a perfect
Dwelling place for the Lord
A splendid and royal palace
To lovingly welcome the Lord

With grace make your house
A temple of the Holy Spirit
Enthroned for ever with
The presence of the Lord

Fr. Robert Hétu

Gift of Freedom

When we were born, God gave us the freedom to choose, right or wrong. There is an ongoing war inside oneself and the challenge is always to honour with what is right. In other words choose the good things in our hearts, so that we can nourish our souls and we will rise and be glorified with God in heaven.

Sometimes humans find that it's really hard to choose right from wrong, especially when we are beside friends and family we want to impress. At these times we should try our hardest to do the right things.

When we were born, God did indeed create us with a soul, we can never run away from our soul. Our soul needs nourishment, from doing good deeds that pleases God.

As Jesus was growing up, He did discovered many of His Powers, one of them was walking on water.

Jesus couldn't hide his true identity from His family or close friends. Not everyone believed in Jesus, but as time went on and they saw what He was like, they believed.

Living Water

(Inspired and adapted from Fr. Richard Hurdle - 1957-2012)

Living Water
My source of hope and healing
Through the pain of my darkness
You reveal Your unconditional love

Living Water
My source of goodness and compassion
Through the shadow of my brokenness
You reveal Yourself to others through me

Living Water
My source of light and becoming
Through the rebirth of my being
You reveal Yourself as the Eternal Presence

Living Water
My source of transformation
Through my pain, brokenness, and rebirth
You reveal the reflection of Your Sacred Image

Living Water
My source of new life and happiness
Through my journey You call others and
You reveal Yourself to a world seeking true life

Fr. Robert Hétu

How do you know God is Communicating with You

God talks to you in different ways: in the next song you hear, the next article you read, the story line of the next movie you watch, the next person you meet, the whisper of a river or an ocean, the next breeze that caresses your face. He will speak to you if you listen and come to you, if you invite Him

However, these are some of the tools in which God communicates with us, yet they are not the only methods, for all feelings and not all thoughts, nor all experiences and not all words written are from God. His words and thoughts are the highest thoughts, the clearest words, your grandest feeling, anything less is from another source. The thoughts from God always contains joy. The clearest words from God are words that contain truth. The greatest feeling is that feeling, which we call Love.

When we listen to Him in these ways. We talk to Him in our prayers, in a wide range of human emotions, we express: joy, excitement, compassion, love, anger, grief, and depression. No matter what we are feeling, God, the Father, wants to hear about it in our prayers. He promises to listen to all our concerns and to answer them for the sake of Jesus.

In the Bible Psalm 1

"Blessed is the man who does not walk in the counsel of the wicked or stand in the way of sinners or sit in the seat of mockers. But his delight is in the law of the Lord."

OTHER IMPORTANT FACTS YOU SHOULD KNOW

Nobody said having Faith would be easy, but it would be worth it and here is why:

- God knows everything we are going through at this very moment and everything we will be going through in the future.

- All things are possible with God.

- God is worthy of our trust.

- God knows what He is doing.

- Let us always follow the **FROG** principle:

  Forever, **R**ely, **O**n, **G**od

Why do children believe in God?

Perhaps, because you are new in this world and your sub-conscience mind knows where you came from, it could be a feeling, no one knows for sure. Children, you have a sense of goodness and you are in search of purpose, always inquisitive and wanting to know all the 'whys' of the world. You are known to have in-depth feelings of things that are trustworthy. Sometimes you cannot express yourselves to an adult, but you know.

Feast of the Passover

(A True Story)

When Jesus was twelve years old, He was allowed to go to Jerusalem with his parents to celebrate the Feast of the Passover. This is the first time He went to Jerusalem and He was so excited to be going to the Temple of His Father's house.

In the Jewish culture, the Feast of the Passover happens every year around the same time as Easter. Directed by God, it started with Moses leading the Israelites out of slavery from Egypt. (Read about this in Exodus 1 in the Bible.)

When the festival was ended and the parents of Jesus started to return, the Boy Jesus stayed behind in Jerusalem at the Temple. Mary and Joseph did not know. After a day's journey, Mary and Joseph could not find Jesus among their family and friends who were also heading back to their homes in Nazareth. Mary and Joseph returned to Jerusalem to find Jesus. After three days they found Him in the Temple sitting among the teachers and rabbis asking questions and in return impressing them with His knowledge.

When Mary saw Jesus, she said "Child, why have you treated us like this?" and continued to say, "Look your father (Joseph) and I have been searching for you with great anxiety."

Then Jesus said to them, "Why were you searching for me? Did you not know that I must be in my Father's house?" Then Jesus went back to Nazareth with His parents and was obedient to them.

Mary treasured all these things in her heart. And Jesus grew up in wisdom and in years, and in divine and human favours.

Mary and Joseph taking the donkey went looking for Jesus.

The Hidden Life of Jesus

As a young boy, Jesus always stayed close to Mary, his mother and Joseph His earthly father. God chose Joseph because he was a carpenter, the highest work on earth to show how much He respected labour. Joseph taught Jesus to become a carpenter too. Jesus worked very hard at being a carpenter in Joseph's shop, that when Joseph died he left it for Jesus to carry on and to take care of His mother, Mary. Jesus was truly a God hidden and passed His years in Eternal wisdom, silence, obedience, prayer and labour. When Jesus was young He gave sight to a blind boy and also healed the sick. To prove to others that He was the Son of God the Father, He healed a possessed man who had evil spirits in him and brought the man back to life. Jesus was kind to everyone that needed His help, **truly God for all.**

With Jesus

(Inspired by a post on Twitter)

Without Jesus, I have no purpose
Without Jesus, I have no direction
Without Jesus, I have no hope
Without Jesus, I have nothing

With Jesus, I have purpose
With Jesus, I have direction
With Jesus, I have hope
With Jesus, I have everything

Amen

Fr. Robert Hétu

www.ingramcontent.com/pod-product-compliance
Lightning Source LLC
Chambersburg PA
CBHW041428120626
46547CB00002B/140